Logic Ladder

A SOLID WAY IN C#

Master SOLID Principles in C# – Write Clean, Robust Code the Fun Way!

HUMNA ANSARI

Includes real-world analogies, refactoring exercises, MCQs, interview prep & a printable cheat sheet!

A student-friendly guide with simple words, real-world logic, and fun examples.

This book is a work of nonfiction created for educational purposes.
All examples, scenarios, and illustrations are original and intended to help readers understand software development concepts.

This edition is distributed through multiple platforms by Draft2Digital.

For inquiries, feedback, or permissions, please contact:
bitzy.logicladder@gmail.com

First Edition

Preface

I've always found it difficult to learn new concepts, especially when explanations are filled with complex jargon and dry theory. With over eight years of software development experience and more than five years of teaching, I've developed a unique way of learning — by making things fun, interactive, and packed with relatable examples. Whenever I tackle a new topic, I collect multiple real-world analogies, break things down into simple terms, and create hands-on exercises to reinforce my understanding. This book is written in the same way I would have loved to learn SOLID principles myself.

Who is this book for?

This book is for all coders like me — those who know how to code in C# and understand Object-Oriented Programming (OOP) but often feel confused about the best practices for writing clean, maintainable code. If you've ever wondered how to structure your code better or struggled with SOLID principles, this book is for you.

What makes this book unique?

Unlike traditional textbooks, this book is not just about theory. It's filled with:

✓ Fun and engaging explanations
✓ Real-life analogies that make complex ideas easy to grasp
✓ Hands-on exercises to apply what you learn
✓ Full code examples so you can follow along
✓ Interview questions to test your understanding and prepare for real-world discussions

What will you learn?

By the end of this book, you'll have a solid understanding of:

- The SOLID principles and why they matter
- Best practices for writing clean, scalable, and maintainable C# code
- How to apply these principles in real-world scenarios

How to use this book?

You can read it cover to cover or jump directly to any principle you want to learn. Each chapter includes exercises to help you practice, with answers provided at the back of the book for self-evaluation.

A Personal Message to My Readers

This book is dedicated to all coders who want to learn but find traditional explanations too difficult and boring. I understand the struggle of deciphering complex tutorials, and that's exactly why I wrote this book — to make learning SOLID principles easy, fun, and practical. Let's dive in and master the art of writing robust C# code together!

TABLE OF CONTENTS

TABLE OF CONTENTS

TABLE OF CONTENTS

Chapter 1

Understanding SOLID Principles

Why Do We Need SOLID?

Imagine you're working on a project that starts off simple. At first, everything seems fine — your code works, and life is good. But as new requirements come in, things start getting messy:

❌ **Making small changes breaks other parts of the code.**
❌ **Fixing one bug creates new ones.**
❌ **Your code becomes a giant, hard-to-maintain mess.**

Sound familiar? This happens because the code lacks proper structure and design principles. **SOLID** was introduced to solve these problems.

What is SOLID?

SOLID is a set of **five principles** that help developers write clean, maintainable, and scalable code. These principles make sure that code is:
✓ **Easy to read** – Other developers (and your future self) can understand it.
✓ **Flexible** – Changes and extensions don't break existing functionality.
✓ **Testable** – Code is structured in a way that allows easy unit testing.

The SOLID principles were introduced by **Robert C. Martin (Uncle Bob)** and are now widely used in software development, especially in **Object-Oriented Programming (OOP).**

These five principles are:

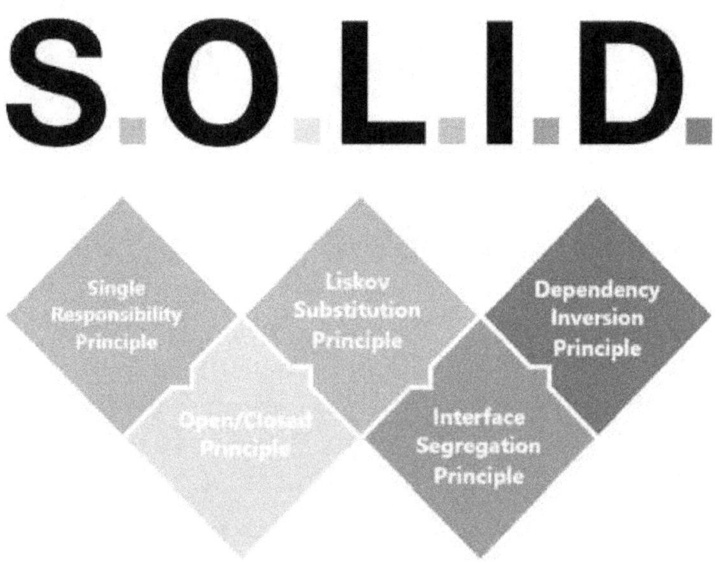

A QUICK LOOK AT EACH SOLID PRINCIPLE

S

Single Responsibility Principle (SRP) – "One Job Only"

Rule: A class should have only one reason to change.

🚫 **Bad Example:** A *ReportGenerator* class that fetches data, formats it, and saves it to a file.

■ **Good Example:** Separate classes: *DataFetcher*, *ReportFormatter*, and *FileSaver*.

O

Open/Closed Principle (OCP) – "Extend, Don't Modify"

Rule: Code should be open for extension, but closed for modification.

🚫 **Bad Example:** You modify an existing *PaymentProcessor* class every time a new payment method is added.

■ **Good Example:** Use separate payment classes that extend a base *PaymentProcessor*.

L

Liskov Substitution Principle (LSP) – "No Surprises"

Rule: Subclasses should be replaceable without breaking the base class behavior.

🚫 **Bad Example:** A *Bird* base class has a *Fly()* method. *Penguin* inherits from *Bird* & throws an error when *Fly()* is called.

■ **Good Example:** Instead, use a separate *FlyingBird* and *NonFlyingBird* class.

I

Interface Segregation Principle (ISP) – "No Unnecessary Dependencies"

Rule: Don't force classes to implement methods they don't use.

🚫 **Bad Example:** A *Worker* interface has *Work()* and *Eat()* methods, but *Robots* implement *Worker* even though they don't eat.

■ **Good Example:** Separate interfaces: *Workable* and *Eatable*.

D

Dependency Inversion Principle (DIP) – "Depend on Abstractions"

Rule: High-level modules should not depend on low-level modules. Both should depend on abstractions.

🚫 **Bad Example:** High-level classes directly depend on low-level classes.

■ **Good Example:** Use interfaces or abstract classes to reduce dependency on concrete implementations.

Real-World Analogy: Divide and Conquer

1. The Overloaded Worker

Imagine you run a restaurant, and one person is responsible for everything:

- Cooking food
- Taking customer orders
- Washing dishes
- Managing finances

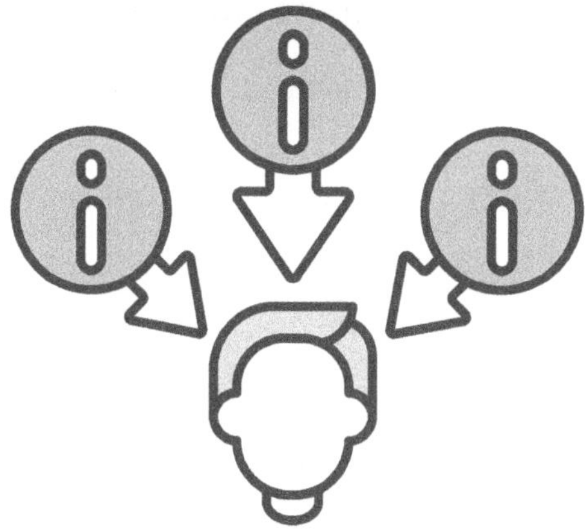

If this person gets overwhelmed, the entire restaurant suffers!
If they leave, everything collapses.

How do successful businesses solve this?

They divide responsibilities:

- A chef cooks.
- A cashier handles payments.
- A server takes orders.

This makes the system efficient, scalable, and manageable—just like well-structured code!

2. The Messy Kitchen

If one kitchen counter is used for chopping vegetables, baking bread, and mixing drinks, it gets cluttered and inefficient. Separating workstations makes the process smoother—just like breaking down classes in code.

3. The Multi-Tasking Robot

Imagine a robot designed to vacuum the floor, wash dishes, and make coffee. If something breaks in the coffee-making system, do you throw away the entire robot? No! You should have separate devices:

- A vacuum for cleaning.
- A dishwasher for washing.
- A coffee machine for brewing.

This is exactly what SRP promotes—separating concerns so that fixing or modifying one part doesn't affect others.

Deep Dive: SRP in Action

Example#1: Handling Reports

Bad Practice: Violating SRP

Let's take an example of a class that handles multiple responsibilities — both the logic for creating a report and the logic for saving it to a file.

```
class ReportGenerator
{
    public void GenerateReport(){
        Console.WriteLine("Generating report...");
    }

    public void SaveReportToFile(string report){
        Console.WriteLine("Saving report to file...");
    }
}
```

Problem:

This class is doing two things:

- Generating a report.
- Saving the report to a file.

If we need to change how the report is saved (for example, saving it to a database instead of a file), we would have to modify this class. This violates SRP because this class has two reasons to change — one for generating the report and one for saving it.

Good Practice: Applying SRP

Now, let's refactor this code to follow SRP. We can split these responsibilities into two separate classes:

```
class ReportGenerator {
    public void GenerateReport() {
        Console.WriteLine("Generating report...");
    }
}

class ReportSaver {
    public void SaveReportToFile(string report) {
        Console.WriteLine("Saving report to file...");
    }
}
```

Benefits:

- **Separation of concerns:** Each class has a clear, single responsibility.
- **Easier to modify and maintain:** If we need to change how we save reports (e.g., saving to a database), we only need to modify *ReportSaver*.
- **Easier to test:** We can now test *ReportGenerator* and *ReportSaver* independently.

Example#2: Handling User Authentication

Bad Practice: Violating SRP

Let's say we have a class that handles user authentication, logs activity, and sends email notifications — all in one place.

```
class UserAuthenticator {
    public bool Login(string username, string password) {
        Console.WriteLine("Checking user credentials...");
        // Authentication logic here
        return true;
    }

    public void LogActivity(string username) {
        Console.WriteLine($"Logging activity for {username}");
    }

    public void SendEmailNotification(string email) {
        Console.WriteLine($"Sending login notification to {email}");
    }
}
```

What's wrong here?

- The class authenticates users ■
- The class logs user activity ✕ (Shouldn't be here)
- The class sends email notifications ✕ (Shouldn't be here)

If we need to change the logging system or modify email notifications, we risk breaking the authentication logic.

Good Practice: Applying SRP

To fix this, let's separate concerns into three focused classes:

```
class UserAuthenticator {
    public bool Login(string username, string password) {
        Console.WriteLine("Checking user credentials...");
        // Authentication logic here
        return true;
    }
}

class ActivityLogger {
    public void LogActivity(string username) {
        Console.WriteLine($"Logging activity for {username}");
    }
}

class EmailNotifier {
    public void SendEmailNotification(string email) {
        Console.WriteLine($"Sending login notification to
{email}");
    }
}
```

Benefits:

- The *UserAuthenticator* class only handles authentication.
- The *ActivityLogger* class manages logging separately.
- The *EmailNotifier* class deals with email notifications independently.
- Easier to modify, test, and reuse these components in different parts of the application.

Conclusion

The Single Responsibility Principle is like organizing a well-run restaurant — every part of the system should focus on a single responsibility. This leads to:

■ Cleaner, more maintainable code
■ Easier debugging and testing
■ Better code reuse

Now Your Turn!

Exercise 1 — Refactor the Code

Problem 1: Order Processing Mess

The *OrderProcessor* class handles order processing, payment, and invoice generation—all in one place. Fix it!

```
class OrderProcessor {
    public void ProcessOrder(string orderId) {
        Console.WriteLine($"Processing order {orderId}");
    }

    public void MakePayment(string orderId, double amount) {
        Console.WriteLine($"Processing payment of ${amount} for order {orderId}");
    }

    public void GenerateInvoice(string orderId) {
        Console.WriteLine($"Generating invoice for order {orderId}");
    }
}
```

◆ Hint: This class is doing three different tasks. Separate them into focused classes.

Problem 2: The Overcomplicated Logger

The *Logger* class is handling both logging messages to a file and sending alerts via email. This violates SRP. Fix it!

```
class Logger {
    public void LogMessage(string message) {
        Console.WriteLine($"Logging message: {message}");
    }

    public void SendEmailAlert(string message) {
        Console.WriteLine($"Sending email alert: {message}");
    }
}
```

◆ Hint: Logging and sending alerts should be separate responsibilities.

Problem 3: The Overloaded Employee Class

The *Employee* class handles employee details, salary calculations, and email notifications. Fix this!

```
class Employee {
    public string Name { get; set; }
    public double Salary { get; set; }

    public void CalculateSalary() {
        Console.WriteLine($"Calculating salary for {Name}");
    }

    public void SendEmailNotification() {
        Console.WriteLine($"Sending email to {Name}");
    }
}
```

◆ Hint: Break it down into smaller, single-purpose classes.

Exercise 2 — Match the Concept

Match each violated principle with the correct fix.

Bad Practice	Correct Solution
1. A class does too many things	A. Separate concerns properly
2. One function handles multiple concerns	B. Keep responsibilities isolated
3. Changing one thing affects others	C. Break it into smaller classes

Exercise 3 — Fill in the Blanks

Complete the sentences with the correct words:

1. SRP states that a class should have only ________ reason(s) to change.
2. Breaking SRP improves ________ and ________ of the code.
3. A ________ class is one that handles multiple concerns instead of just one.

Exercise 4 — Multiple Choice Questions (MCQs)

. What is the main goal of SRP?
A) To reduce the number of classes.
B) To make each class handle multiple responsibilities
C) To ensure each class has only one reason to change
D) To improve execution speed.

2. Which of these violates SRP?
A) A class that only authenticates users
B) A class that both calculates salary and sends salary emails
C) A class that logs errors separately from error handling
D) A class that follows modular design

Interview Questions for SRP

. What is the Single Responsibility Principle (SRP)?

◆ **Answer:** SRP states that a class should have only one reason to change, meaning it should have only one responsibility.

. Why is SRP important?

◆ **Answer:** It improves code maintainability, readability, and flexibility by ensuring that changes in one responsibility do not affect other unrelated functionalities.

. How do you identify SRP violations?

◆ **Answer:** If a class handles multiple, unrelated tasks (e.g., handling database operations, UI rendering, and business logic in one class), it's violating SRP.

. What happens if SRP is not followed?

◆ **Answer:** The code becomes hard to modify, tightly coupled, and prone to unexpected bugs because a change in one area might break another.

. How do you fix an SRP violation?

◆ **Answer:** Break the class into multiple smaller classes, each handling a single responsibility. For example, instead of a *ReportManager* doing everything, create *ReportGenerator*, *ReportPrinter*, and *ReportEmailSender* separately.

. Can a class have multiple methods and still follow SRP?

◆ **Answer:** Yes, as long as all methods contribute to one single responsibility.

. What is the difference between SRP and modular programming?

◆ **Answer:**

- SRP is a design principle ensuring each class has only one responsibility.
- Modular programming is a broader concept where code is divided into separate, independent modules, which may still contain SRP-violating classes inside them.

. How does SRP help in writing unit tests?

◆ **Answer:** SRP ensures small, focused classes, making it easier to write isolated unit tests for each responsibility without dependencies on unrelated code.

. Can SRP be applied to methods as well?

◆ **Answer:** Yes! A method should do only one thing. If a method performs multiple tasks, split it into smaller methods for better readability and maintainability.

10. How does SRP relate to microservices architecture?

◆ **Answer:** Microservices follow the same idea as SRP but at a system level. Each microservice handles only one business capability, just like SRP ensures each class has only one responsibility.

Chapter 3

Open/Closed Principle (OCP)

What is OCP?

The **Open/Closed Principle (OCP)** states that:

> ***Software entities (such as classes, modules, functions) should be open for extension but closed for modification.***

This means you should be able to **add new functionality** without modifying existing code. Instead of altering a working class when adding new features, you should extend it using **inheritance, interfaces, or composition.**
Think of it like a power strip 🔌 — you can plug in new devices without rewiring the entire electrical system!

Why OCP Matters

A well-designed system should be flexible enough to accommodate changes without breaking existing functionality. When you follow OCP:
■ You reduce bugs by avoiding direct modifications to working code.
■ Your system becomes scalable, allowing new features to be added easily.
■ Your code remains maintainable, as changes are localized to new classes instead of affecting existing logic.

Problems Caused by Violating OCP

■ **Frequent modifications lead to unstable code –** Every time you change a class, there's a risk of breaking existing functionality.
■ **Harder to scale –** Adding new features means modifying existing classes, leading to tightly coupled code.
■ **Difficult maintenance –** When different concerns are mixed into one class, understanding and updating the code becomes a nightmare.

When OCP is Broken: Common Signs

How do you know if your code violates OCP? Look for these warning signs:

● Constant modifications to existing classes whenever a new feature is added.
● A large class with too many responsibilities (violates SRP too).
● Lots of if-else or switch statements for different behaviors, making it hard to introduce new variations.
● High risk of breaking functionality when adding new requirements.

Real-World Analogy: Open for More, Closed for Changes

1. Smartphone Apps – Adding Features Without Changing the Phone

Imagine you own a smartphone. Initially, it comes with basic features like calling and texting. But as new needs arise, you can install new apps instead of modifying the phone's core software.
■ New Features? Install a new app.
✕ Not Needed? Uninstall it without affecting the system.
This follows OCP because:

- The **phone's software is closed for modification** (you don't rewrite its OS for every new feature).
- The **system is open for extension** through apps (new features are added via external applications).

2. Power Sockets – Open for More, Closed for Changes

Think about the power sockets in your house. They have a standard design that doesn't change over time. But you can always add power adapters, extensions, and different plug types based on your needs.
🔌 Want to charge more devices? Use a power strip.
🔌 Need an international plug? Use an adapter.
The **core socket remains unchanged** (closed for modification), but it allows extensions (open for adding functionality).

3. Video Game DLCs – Expanding the Game Without Modifying Core Mechanics

Many video games release DLCs (Downloadable Content). Instead of modifying the base game, new levels, characters, or missions are added as extensions.
🎮 Original game stays intact.
🎮New content (characters, maps, challenges) is added without breaking the existing game.
This aligns with OCP because:
■ The game doesn't require changes in the core system.
■ Developers simply extend the functionality by adding new content.

These real-world scenarios illustrate how OCP ensures scalability and flexibility without altering existing functionality.

Deep Dive: OCP in Action

Example#1: Payment Processing System

Let's say we are building a **payment processing system**. Initially, our system only supports credit card payments. Later, we decide to **add more payment methods** like PayPal and Bitcoin.

Bad Practice: Violating OCP

A *PaymentProcessor* class is created to handle payments:

```
public class PaymentProcessor
{
    public void ProcessPayment(string paymentType, double amount)
    {
        if (paymentType == "CreditCard")
        {
            Console.WriteLine($"Processing credit card payment of ${amount}");
        }
        else if (paymentType == "PayPal")
        {
            Console.WriteLine($"Processing PayPal payment of ${amount}");
        }
        else if (paymentType == "Bitcoin")
        {
            Console.WriteLine($"Processing Bitcoin payment of ${amount}");
        }
    }
}
```

Why does this violate OCP?

- Every time a new payment method is added, we have to modify the PaymentProcessor class.
- This increases the risk of breaking existing code.
- The class is not closed for modification because changes are required each time a new feature is added.

Good Practice: Applying OCP with Abstraction

Instead of modifying the existing class, let's create an abstract *PaymentMethod* class and extend functionality without modifying the existing code.

Step 1: Create an abstract class for PaymentMethod

```
public abstract class PaymentMethod
{
    public abstract void ProcessPayment(double amount);
}
```

Quick Reminder!

An **abstract class** is a class that cannot be directly used to create objects. It only provides a blueprint for other classes to follow. It can have abstract methods *(which must be implemented by child classes)* and regular methods *(which can be shared by all child classes).*

💡 Think of it like a template that other classes must complete!

Step 2: Create Concrete Classes for Each Payment Method

```
public class CreditCardPayment : PaymentMethod
{
    public override void ProcessPayment(double amount)  {
        Console.WriteLine($"Processing credit card payment of ${amount}");
    }
}

public class PayPalPayment : PaymentMethod
{
    public override void ProcessPayment(double amount)  {
        Console.WriteLine($"Processing PayPal payment of ${amount}");
    }
}
```

Step 3: Use OCP-friendly design in the PaymentProcessor

```
public class PaymentProcessor
{
    public void ProcessPayment(PaymentMethod paymentMethod, double amount)
    {
        paymentMethod.ProcessPayment(amount);
    }
}
```

Step 4: Calling the PaymentProcessor in Main

```
class Program
{
    static void Main()
    {
        PaymentProcessor processor = new PaymentProcessor();

        // Using different payment methods
        PaymentMethod creditCard = new CreditCardPayment();
        PaymentMethod payPal = new PayPalPayment();
        PaymentMethod bitcoin = new BitcoinPayment();

        processor.ProcessPayment(creditCard, 100.00);
        processor.ProcessPayment(payPal, 50.00);
        processor.ProcessPayment(bitcoin, 200.00);
    }
}
```

◆ Now, adding a new payment method (e.g., Apple Pay) is easy!
Just create a new class:

```
public class ApplePayPayment : PaymentMethod
{
    public override void ProcessPayment(double amount)
    {
        Console.WriteLine($"Processing Apple Pay payment of ${amount}");
    }
}
```

Why is this design better?

- *PaymentProcessor* does not need to be modified when adding new payment methods.
- New payment methods (e.g., *ApplePayPayment*) can be added without touching existing code.
- Code follows OCP by being open for extension, closed for modification.

Example#2: Discount Calculator

Let's say we have a *DiscountCalculator* class that calculates discounts for different customer types.

Bad Practice: Violating OCP

```
public class DiscountCalculator
{
    public double GetDiscount(string customerType, double price)
    {
        if (customerType == "Regular"){
            return price * 0.10; // 10% discount
        }
        else if (customerType == "Premium"){
            return price * 0.20; // 20% discount
        }
        else if (customerType == "VIP"){
            return price * 0.30; // 30% discount
        }
        return 0; // No discount
    }
}
```

Why does this violate OCP?

- Every time a new customer type is added, we must modify this class.
- This violates OCP because we are modifying existing code instead of extending it.
- If we forget to update the class, it may cause bugs in the discount system.

Good Practice: Applying OCP with Abstraction

We will apply OCP by using inheritance and polymorphism. Instead of modifying *DiscountCalculator*, we create separate discount classes.

Step 1: Create an abstract class for Discounts

```
public abstract class Discount
{
    public abstract double ApplyDiscount(double price);
}
```

Step 2: Create specific Discount Classes

```
public class RegularDiscount : Discount
{
    public override double ApplyDiscount(double price) => price * 0.10;
}

public class PremiumDiscount : Discount
{
    public override double ApplyDiscount(double price) => price * 0.20;
}

public class VIPDiscount : Discount
{
    public override double ApplyDiscount(double price) => price * 0.30;
}
```

Do you know?

```
public override double ApplyDiscount(double price) => price * 0.10;
```

This is a shortcut **(expression-bodied method)** for:

```
public override double ApplyDiscount(double price)
{
    return price * 0.10;
}
```

Step 3: Use the discount strategy

```
public class DiscountCalculator
{
    public double GetDiscount(Discount discount, double price){
        return discount.ApplyDiscount(price);
    }
}
```

Step 4: Calling the Discount Calculator in Main

```
class Program
{
    static void Main()
    {
        DiscountCalculator calculator = new DiscountCalculator();

        Discount regular = new RegularDiscount();
        Discount premium = new PremiumDiscount();
        Discount vip = new VIPDiscount();

        double price = 100;

        Console.WriteLine("Regular Discount: " + calculator.GetDiscount(regular, price));  // 10% off
        Console.WriteLine("Premium Discount: " + calculator.GetDiscount(premium, price)); // 20% off
        Console.WriteLine("VIP Discount: " + calculator.GetDiscount(vip, price));         // 30% off
    }
}
```

Why is this a good practice?

- We don't modify existing code when adding a new customer type.
- We extend functionality by simply adding a new class.
- Code is more readable, scalable, and maintainable.

Conclusion

The Open/Closed Principle ensures that our code is open for extension but closed for modification. By structuring our classes to be easily extendable, we reduce the risk of breaking existing functionality while adding new features.

Key Takeaways:

✓ **Prevents breaking changes –** Existing code remains untouched when adding new functionality.
✓ **Encourages scalability –** Easily extend behavior without modifying the base logic.
✓ **Promotes maintainability –** Code stays modular, readable, and adaptable.

By following OCP, you can build software that adapts to change gracefully without introducing unnecessary risks. Now, let's test your understanding with some exercises! 🚀

Now Your Turn!

Exercise 1 — Refactor the Code

Problem 1: Discount & Invoice Generation

The following code violates both SRP and OCP. Refactor it to follow both principles.

```
public class Invoice
{
    public double CalculateTotal(double price, int quantity, string customerType)
    {
        double discount = 0;

        if (customerType == "Regular")
            discount = price * 0.05;
        else if (customerType == "Premium")
            discount = price * 0.10;

        double total = (price * quantity) - discount;
        Console.WriteLine("Invoice Generated: " + total);
        return total;
    }
}
```

◆ Hint: Separate concerns by handling discount logic and invoice generation separately.

Problem 2: Area Calculator

The following code violates the Open/Closed Principle by requiring modifications for every new shape. Refactor it to follow OCP.

```
public class AreaCalculator
{
    public double CalculateArea(object shape)
    {
        if (shape is Circle)
        {
            Circle c = (Circle)shape;
            return Math.PI * c.Radius * c.Radius;
        }
        else if (shape is Rectangle)
        {
            Rectangle r = (Rectangle)shape;
            return r.Width * r.Height;
        }
        return 0;
    }
}
```

◆ Hint: Use polymorphism instead of conditionals.

Exercise 2 — Match the Concept

Match the OCP-related concepts with their correct explanations.

Concept	Explanation
1. Open/Closed Principle	A. Using if-else conditions to handle new cases instead of extending behavior.
2. Violation of OCP	B. Applying abstraction and polymorphism to allow future extensions.
3. Solution for OCP	C. Existing code should remain unchanged while allowing extensions.

Exercise 3 — Fill in the Blanks

Complete the sentences with the correct words:

1. OCP states that a class should be ________ for extension but ________ for modification.
2. The key technique to implement OCP is using ________ and ________ instead of modifying existing code.
3. Using a ________ class allows behavior to be extended without changing base logic.

Exercise 4 — Multiple Choice Questions (MCQs)

1. Which of the following violates the Open/Closed Principle?
A) Using interfaces for different behaviors
B) Adding new conditions inside an existing method
C) Using polymorphism to override behavior
D) Extending functionality by creating new classes

2. Which design pattern is commonly used to follow OCP?
A) Singleton
B) Factory Method
C) Strategy
D) Observer

Interview Questions for OCP

. What does the Open/Closed Principle (OCP) state?

◆ **Answer:** OCP states that a class should be open for extension but closed for modification.

. Why is it important to follow the Open/Closed Principle in software design?

◆ **Answer:** It allows new functionality to be added without altering existing code, reducing bugs and improving maintainability.

. How does violating OCP affect code maintainability and scalability?

◆ **Answer:** Modifying existing code can introduce new bugs and make it harder to scale the application.

. What are some common signs that a class violates OCP?

◆ **Answer:** If a class is frequently modified to accommodate new features, it likely violates OCP.

. How can abstraction help in achieving OCP?

◆ **Answer:** Abstract classes and interfaces allow new behaviors to be added without changing existing implementations.

. What is the main difference between OCP and SRP?

◆ **Answer:** SRP ensures a class has only one responsibility, while OCP ensures it can be extended without modification.

. How can polymorphism be used to implement OCP?

◆ **Answer:** By defining a base class or interface and allowing new subclasses to extend functionality without modifying the base code.

. What are some real-world examples where OCP is useful?

◆ **Answer:** Payment processing systems, where new payment methods can be added without modifying existing code.

. How do interfaces or abstract classes help in following OCP?

◆ **Answer:** They define a common contract, allowing new implementations to be added without changing the existing system.

10. What are the disadvantages of using OCP? Can it lead to excessive class creation?

◆ **Answer:** Yes, if not managed properly, OCP can lead to too many small classes, increasing complexity.

Interview Questions for OCP

1. **How does the Strategy Pattern relate to OCP?**

◆ **Answer:** The Strategy Pattern allows new behaviors to be added by defining interchangeable strategies, following OCP.

1 . **Can you explain a scenario where applying OCP led to better software design?**

◆ **Answer:** A logging system where new log formats (e.g., JSON, XML) were added using separate classes without modifying existing code.

1 . **How does OCP interact with Dependency Injection?**

◆ **Answer:** Dependency Injection allows injecting new implementations at runtime without modifying dependent classes.

1 . **What trade-offs should developers consider when applying OCP?**

◆ **Answer:** Overuse of abstraction can make code harder to understand and maintain. Balance is key.

1 . **How would you refactor a legacy system that violates OCP?**

◆ **Answer:** Identify frequently changing code, introduce abstraction (interfaces or base classes), and extract new functionality into separate classes.

Chapter 4

Liskov Substitution Principle (LSP)

What is LSP?

The **Liskov Substitution Principle (LSP)** states that:

> ***A subclass should be replaceable for its base class without breaking the program.***

In simple words, if a class is inherited from another class, it should be able to stand in for the parent class **without changing the expected behavior.**
💡 Think of it this way:
If a function is working fine with a parent class, it should also work fine if you pass a child class—without causing errors or unexpected behavior.

Why LSP Matters

LSP ensures that your code remains **predictable, flexible, and reusable.** If a subclass does not behave like its parent, it can lead to **unexpected bugs, incorrect outputs, or even crashes** when the wrong object is used.
◆ Benefits of following LSP:
■Helps maintain code consistency
■Reduces runtime errors caused by incompatible classes
■Makes the codebase easier to extend and refactor

Problems Caused by Violating LSP

When LSP is violated, subclasses behave differently from their base class, breaking existing code. This can lead to serious issues, such as:

❌ **Unexpected Errors & Bugs** – The code might assume a subclass works exactly like its parent, but if it changes expected behavior, it can cause unexpected crashes or incorrect results.
❌ **Unreliable Inheritance** – Instead of making reuse easier, extending a class may introduce hidden issues, forcing developers to constantly adjust their code to handle exceptions.
❌ **Hard-to-Maintain Code** – When a subclass does not truly follow its parent's behavior, developers have to add extra conditions (if checks, type casts, workarounds), leading to a tangled, messy codebase.
❌ **Inconsistent Behavior Across the Codebase** – Different parts of the code might expect an object to behave in a certain way, but if a subclass alters that behavior, it can cause confusion and make debugging difficult.
By ensuring subclasses remain true to their parent class behavior, we can write **stable, predictable, and maintainable code.** ■

When LSP is Broken: Common Signs

How can you tell if a class violates LSP? Look for these common signs:

🔴 **Subclasses throw unexpected errors**

- If a subclass overrides a method but cannot fulfill its contract, it might throw exceptions instead.

🚨 **Example**: Imagine a *Bird* class that has a *Fly()* method. If we create a *Penguin* subclass, **it cannot fly,** which violates LSP because it breaks the expected behavior of the base class.

🔴 **Subclasses ignore or override essential behaviors**

- If a subclass disables or modifies a parent method in a way that changes expected behavior, it's an LSP violation.

🚨 **Example:** A *BaseLogger* class has a *LogMessage()* method. If a *NullLogger* subclass overrides it **to do nothing**, the expected logging behavior is broken.

🔴 **Clients need to check the object type before using it**

- If you find yourself using if statements to check if an object is a subclass before calling a method, LSP is likely violated.

🚨 **Example:**

```
if (shape is Square)
{
    // Handle it differently
}
else
{
    // Normal case
}
```

This defeats the purpose of **polymorphism**. Instead of relying on inheritance, we are adding **manual conditions,** making the code harder to maintain.

🔴 **A Method Throws Unexpected Errors**

- If a subclass overrides a method but throws an error instead of executing expected behavior, it likely violates LSP.

📌 **Example:**

If a Bird class has a *Fly()* method and a *Penguin* subclass throws an exception *(NotImplementedException)*, it means the subclass does not conform to the base class behavior. This is a clear violation of LSP.

✅ **Better Approach:**

Instead of forcing all birds to implement *Fly()*, we should create separate classes:

- *FlyingBird* with a *Fly()* method
- *NonFlyingBird* without *Fly()*

Now, penguins won't break expectations! 🐧

Real-World Analogy: Subclasses That Just Work

1. Broken Promises in a Restaurant

Imagine you visit a restaurant that offers online food ordering. They promise:

- "Order online, and we will deliver in 30 minutes!"

You place an order, but instead of delivering to your home, they send you a message:

■ *"Sorry, we don't deliver to homes. You need to pick up your order from our branch."*

This is frustrating because they broke the promise they made on their website. Their service did not behave as expected when extended to deliveries.

✕ How This Violates LSP

In object-oriented terms:

The restaurant initially acted like a base class (*FoodOrderingService*) that promised home delivery. But when you interacted with the actual subclass (*SpecificRestaurantService*), it failed to honor the contract and changed how things worked.

This is exactly what happens when a subclass overrides behavior in a way that breaks expectations, violating LSP.

2. Electric Cars vs. Gas Cars

Imagine you own a car rental company. You offer both gasoline cars and electric cars.

Your app has a simple method for all cars:

car.Refuel();

Now, a customer rents a Tesla (ElectricCar) and tries to refuel it using the same method.

● *Problem: A Tesla doesn't use gasoline! Calling Refuel() on an electric car doesn't make sense, and the method is either:*

- *Not implemented, causing an error* ✕

Misleadingly implemented to do something unrelated, like "charging" the car ■

✕ How This Violates LSP

- The base class *Car* assumes that all cars can be refueled.
- The subclass *ElectricCar* changes the expected behavior by not supporting fuel.
- This breaks LSP because *ElectricCar* cannot be substituted everywhere a Car is used.

■ Better Approach:

Instead of forcing all cars to implement Refuel(), split them into separate interfaces.

```
interface IGasCar { void Refuel(); }
interface IElectricCar { void Charge(); }
```

Now, each type of car follows the correct contract without violating LSP! ●

Deep Dive: LSP in Action

Example#1: Penguin As a Bird

Imagine a *Bird* class with a method *Fly()*. Now, we create a subclass *Penguin*, which cannot fly.

Bad Practice: Violating LSP

Misusing Inheritance

```
class Bird
{
    public virtual void Fly()
    {
        Console.WriteLine("Flying high in the sky!");
    }
}

class Penguin : Bird
{
    public override void Fly()
    {
        throw new Exception("Penguins cannot fly!");
    }
}
```

Why does this violate LSP?

- The *Penguin* class changes the behavior of *Fly()* by throwing an exception.
- Any code expecting all *Bird* objects to be able to fly will **break** when it encounters a *Penguin*.

Good Practice: Use Proper Abstraction

Instead of forcing all birds to fly, we separate flying and non-flying birds.

Step 1: Define the Base Class

```
abstract class Bird
{
    public abstract void MakeSound();
}
```

Step 2: Create Derived Classes for Flying and Non-Flying Birds

```
class FlyingBird : Bird
{
    public void Fly()  {
        Console.WriteLine("Flying high in the sky!");
    }

    public override void MakeSound()  {
        Console.WriteLine("Chirp Chirp!");
    }
}
class NonFlyingBird : Bird
{
    public void Walk()  {
        Console.WriteLine("Walking on the ground!");
    }

    public override void MakeSound()  {
        Console.WriteLine("Honk Honk!");
    }
}
```

Quick Reminder!

A **Derived Class** is a class that inherits from another class (called the base class). It reuses the properties and methods of the base class while adding its own unique behavior.

Here, *Penguin* inherits from *Bird*, so it can use *MakeSound()*, but it also adds its own method *Swim()*.

✓ ***Key Benefit:*** Code reuse—no need to rewrite common functionality! 🚀

Step 3: Create Derived Classes for Specific Birds

```
class Penguin : NonFlyingBird
{
    public void Swim()
    {
        Console.WriteLine("Swimming in the ocean!");
    }
}

class Ostrich : NonFlyingBird
{
    public void RunFast()
    {
        Console.WriteLine("Running fast in the wild!");
    }
}
```

Step 4: Call it in Main

```
class Program
{
    static void Main()
    {
        FlyingBird sparrow = new FlyingBird();
        sparrow.MakeSound();
        sparrow.Fly();

        NonFlyingBird ostrich = new Ostrich();
        ostrich.MakeSound();
        ostrich.Walk();

        NonFlyingBird penguin = new Penguin();
        penguin.MakeSound();
        penguin.Walk();
        ((Penguin)penguin).Swim(); // Specific to Penguin
    }
}
```

Why is this a good practice?

- Clear separation between flying and non-flying birds.
- No broken behaviors (No bird is forced to have a *Fly()* method it doesn't need).
- Easier expansion (We can add more flightless birds like Kiwis without changing existing code).

What if we create a object specific to Penguin. In this way, we will be able to call all its methods and parent class method?

Yes, exactly! If you create an object specifically for *Penguin*, you won't need to cast it to call its *Swim()* method. Here's how it works:

Without Casting (Direct Penguin Object)

```
Penguin penguin = new Penguin();
penguin.MakeSound();  // Inherited from NonFlyingBird
penguin.Walk();       // Inherited from NonFlyingBird
penguin.Swim();       // Specific to Penguin
```

■ **No casting required!**

Since penguin is already a *Penguin* object, it inherits from *NonFlyingBird* and also has its own unique method *Swim()*.

But Why Did We Use a Parent Reference?

```
NonFlyingBird penguin = new Penguin();
penguin.MakeSound();
penguin.Walk();
((Penguin)penguin).Swim();  // Casting required
```

Here, penguin is declared as a *NonFlyingBird*. This means:

✓ It can access all methods from *NonFlyingBird*.

✗ But it doesn't know about *Swim()* (which belongs to *Penguin*).

✓ So we cast it to *Penguin* to access *Swim()*.

Which One Should You Use?

- **Use the parent class reference**
  (NonFlyingBird penguin = new Penguin();)

■ When you only need common behaviors shared by all non-flying birds.

■ This is useful in polymorphism, when you work with a list of different birds.

- **Use the specific class**
  (Penguin penguin = new Penguin();)

■ When you need access to all Penguin-specific methods without casting.

■ This is best when you're sure the object is always a Penguin.

Final Takeaway

Both approaches are correct, but they serve different purposes:

✓ **Polymorphism (parent reference)** → More flexibility, but needs casting.

✓ **Direct object creation (specific reference)** → No casting, but less flexible.

Example#2: Electric and Gas Cars

Imagine you are designing a system for different types of cars.

Bad Practice: Violating LSP

You start with a base class *Car* that includes a method for *Refueling*. Now, you create a subclass *ElectricCar*, which extends *Car*:

```
class Car
{
    public virtual void Refuel()
    {
        Console.WriteLine("Car is refueling at a gas station.");
    }
}
class ElectricCar : Car
{
    public override void Refuel()
    {
        throw new NotImplementedException("Electric cars do not
refuel with gas!");
    }
}
```

Quick Reminder!

A **virtual method** is a method in a base class that can be overridden in a derived class. It allows subclasses to provide their own implementation while keeping the same method signature.

The **override** keyword is used in a derived class to replace the behavior of a virtual method from the base class.

Why does this violate LSP?

- The *ElectricCar* inherits *Refuel()* but cannot use it properly.
- Code expecting a *Car* might call *Refuel()*, but it breaks for electric cars.
- This violates Liskov Substitution Principle (LSP) because *ElectricCar* cannot fully replace *Car* without unexpected failures.

Good Practice: Use Interfaces

Instead of forcing all cars to have *Refuel()*, we can split them into two interfaces:

Step 1: Create separate interfaces

```
interface IGasCar
{
    void Refuel();
}

interface IElectricCar
{
    void Recharge();
}
```

Step 2: Define Specific Classes

```
class GasCar : IGasCar
{
    public void Refuel()  {
        Console.WriteLine("Gas car is refueling at a gas station.");
    }
}
class ElectricCar : IElectricCar
{
    public void Recharge()  {
        Console.WriteLine("Electric car is charging at a station.");
    }
}
```

Step 3: Calling it in Main

```
class Program
{
    static void Main()
    {
        IGasCar myGasCar = new GasCar();
        myGasCar.Refuel();

        IElectricCar myElectricCar = new
ElectricCar();
        myElectricCar.Recharge();
    }
}
```

Why is this a good practice?

- No *NotImplementedException* — each class has only relevant behavior.
- A *GasCar* can be used anywhere an *IGasCar* is expected.
- An *ElectricCar* can be used anywhere an *IElectricCar* is expected.
- Follows LSP — subtypes behave correctly without breaking expectations.

What if during designing of program there was no concept for the Electric Cars and all cars wanted fuel, so we placed Fuel method in a base class. Suddenly electric cars come into the market and our program is failing. Now, we can't modify existing code. How will we deal with electric cars then?

That's a great question! If electric cars were introduced later, and modifying the existing Car class and its subclasses would break the system, we can handle this without violating LSP using the **Adapter Pattern.**
Instead of modifying the existing Car class, we create an adapter that allows electric cars to be treated like fuel-based cars without breaking existing code.

Existing Code (Before Electric Cars)

```
class Car
{
    public virtual void Refuel()
    {
        Console.WriteLine("Car is refueling at a gas station.");
    }
}
```

Adapter for Electric Cars

Since electric cars don't use fuel, we create an adapter that "translates" *Refuel()* into *Recharge()*, keeping the existing system intact.

```
class ElectricCarAdapter : Car
{
    private ElectricCar electricCar;

    public ElectricCarAdapter(ElectricCar car)
    {
        electricCar = car;
    }

    public override void Refuel()
    {
        Console.WriteLine("Electric car doesn't refuel. Redirecting to recharge.");
        electricCar.Recharge();
    }
}
```

ElectricCar Class

```
class ElectricCar
{
    public void Recharge()
    {
        Console.WriteLine("Electric car is charging at a station.");
    }
}
```

Calling in Main()

```
class Program
{
    static void Main()
    {
        Car myFuelCar = new Car();
        myFuelCar.Refuel();  // Works as usual

        ElectricCar myElectricCar = new ElectricCar();
        Car electricAdapter = new ElectricCarAdapter(myElectricCar);
        electricAdapter.Refuel();  // Calls Recharge() internally
    }
}
```

Why This Works?

✔ No need to modify the Car class, avoiding breaking changes.

✔ The system still expects all cars to have *Refuel()*, but the adapter redirects it to *Recharge()* for electric cars.

✔ LSP is preserved—electric cars behave as expected without unexpected crashes.

Conclusion

The Liskov Substitution Principle is all about trust – trusting that a subclass will behave just like its parent. When this trust is broken, our code can become unpredictable, hard to maintain, and full of bugs.
By following LSP, we ensure that:
- Subclasses can stand in for their parent classes without causing issues
- Inheritance stays clean, reliable, and reusable
- Our applications remain flexible and easier to extend in the future

In short, LSP helps us write code that's robust, predictable, and future-proof. Now that you've got this principle in your toolkit, you're one step closer to mastering clean software design!

Now Your Turn!

Exercise 1 **Refactor the Code**

Problem 1: Report Generator

The following code violates the Liskov Substitution Principle. See if you can spot and fix it.

```
public class ReportGenerator
{
    public virtual void GenerateReport()
    {
        Console.WriteLine("Generating report...");
    }
}

public class ExcelReportGenerator : ReportGenerator
{
    public override void GenerateReport()
    {
        Console.WriteLine("Generating Excel report...");
    }
}

public class ReadOnlyReport : ReportGenerator
{
    public override void GenerateReport()
    {
        throw new NotImplementedException("This report is read-only and cannot be generated.");
    }
}

class Program
{
    static void Main()
    {
        List<ReportGenerator> reports = new List<ReportGenerator>
        {
            new ExcelReportGenerator(),
            new ReadOnlyReport()
        };

        foreach (var report in reports)
        {
            report.GenerateReport();
        }
    }
}
```

✎Task:

- This code breaks LSP. Can you explain why?
- Refactor the code so that *ReadOnlyReport* doesn't break substitutability. Use proper abstraction.

Problem 2: Manage User Class

The following code is trying to manage user data and also send emails. But something's wrong here.

```
public class User
{
    public string Name { get; set; }
    public string Email { get; set; }

    public virtual void SaveUser()
    {
        Console.WriteLine("Saving user to database...");
    }

    public virtual void SendWelcomeEmail()
    {
        Console.WriteLine("Sending welcome email to " + Email);
    }
}

public class GuestUser : User
{
    public override void SendWelcomeEmail()
    {
        // Guest users shouldn't receive emails
        throw new NotImplementedException("Guest users don't get welcome emails.");
    }
}
```

✎Task:

- Can you spot how this violates Liskov Substitution Principle?
- Also, can you identify how it breaks Single Responsibility Principle?
- Refactor this design to fix both issues.

Exercise 2 Match the Concept

Match each violated principle with the correct fix.

Concept	Explanation
1. Liskov Substitution Principle	A. Subclass throws exception for a method in base class
2. Virtual Method	B. A principle that ensures subclasses can be used in place of base classes without surprises.
3. Override Keyword	C. Allows a method to be overridden in derived class
4. Broken Substitution	D. Helps split incompatible behaviors cleanly
5. Refactoring with Interfaces	E. Used in derived class to modify base class method behavior

Exercise 3 Fill in the Blanks

Fill in the blanks with the correct terms from the list below:

(subclass, override, behavior, LSP, base class)

1. The _____ should be replaceable by its ______ without changing the program's expected ______.
2. Violating ______ can result in unexpected bugs and fragile code.
3. If a subclass needs to change how a method works, it can use the ______ keyword.

Exercise 4 Match the Concept

1. What is the main idea behind the Liskov Substitution Principle?

A) All classes should inherit from a single base class

B) Subclasses should be used only for adding new methods

C) Objects of a subclass should be replaceable for objects of a base class without affecting the program

D) Subclasses must always override all methods of the parent class

2. Which situation would likely violate LSP?

A) A class follows the Open/Closed Principle

B) A subclass throws an exception for a method expected to work

C) A method is overridden to improve performance

D) A class uses dependency injection

3. What is a common result of violating LSP in your codebase?

A) Reduced lines of code

B) Clearer hierarchy

C) Unexpected behavior and bugs

D) Faster execution

4. Which of the following helps ensure LSP is not violated?

A) Using static methods only

B) Avoiding inheritance altogether

C) Designing subclasses that follow the contract of the base class

D) Making all methods private

Interview Questions for LSP

. What is the Liskov Substitution Principle (LSP)?
◆ **Answer:** It states that objects of a subclass should be able to replace objects of a base class without affecting the program's correctness.

. How can LSP violations affect your code?
◆ **Answer:** It can introduce unexpected bugs when a subclass behaves differently, breaking the assumptions made in the base class.

. Give a real-life analogy of LSP.
◆ **Answer:** If a bird can fly, all its subclasses (like sparrow, pigeon) should also be able to fly. But if you add penguin as a subclass and it can't fly, it breaks expectations.

. Can you mention a sign that LSP is broken in your code?
◆ **Answer:** If you find yourself adding *if* conditions to check the type of subclass before using it, that's a red flag.

. How is LSP related to polymorphism?
◆ **Answer:** LSP ensures that polymorphism works correctly by guaranteeing that subclasses honor the behavior of the base class.

. How do you fix an LSP violation?
◆ **Answer:** By restructuring the class hierarchy — use better abstraction, break down classes, or use interfaces where needed.

. Why does overriding a method with different behavior break LSP?
◆ **Answer:** Because it changes the expected outcome of the method defined in the base class, which can lead to bugs when used polymorphically.

. How does LSP help in writing maintainable code?
◆ **Answer:** It ensures subclasses behave predictably, so you can safely reuse and extend code without unexpected side effects.

. Can you give an example where inheritance should be avoided to preserve LSP?
◆ **Answer:** If *Square* extends *Rectangle* but changes how width and height work, it breaks LSP. In such cases, prefer composition over inheritance.

10. **What's the difference between following LSP and just having correct inheritance?**
◆ **Answer:** Correct inheritance means subclassing syntactically; following LSP ensures behavior consistency so that subclasses don't surprise the code that uses them.

Interface Segregation Principle (ISP)

What is ISP?

The **Interface Segregation Principle (ISP)** says:

> ***Clients should not be forced to depend on interfaces they do not use.***

In simple words, **don't make a class implement a huge interface with methods it doesn't need**. Instead, **split large interfaces into smaller, more specific ones**, so that classes only implement what they actually need.

Why ISP Matters

When we force a class to implement unnecessary methods, we create messy and confusing code. It leads to:

- Extra code with empty or misleading implementations
- More chances of bugs when changes are made
- Difficulties in maintaining and understanding the system

By following ISP, we keep code clean, **focused**, and **flexible**.

Problems Caused by Violating ISP

When we break the Interface Segregation Principle, we often see:
❌ Classes implementing methods that don't make sense for them
❌ Dummy method implementations just to satisfy the interface
❌ Confusion when other developers try to use or extend the code
❌ Tightly coupled design that's hard to change or reuse

When ISP is Broken: Common Signs

Here are some signs that your code might be violating the Interface Segregation Principle:
🔍 **Empty or Throwing Methods :** If a class implements an interface but has methods that are empty or throw *NotImplementedException*, that's a clear red flag.

🔍 **Too Many Irrelevant Methods :** The interface forces a class to implement too many things it doesn't need — making the code noisy and confusing.

🔍 **Unrelated Responsibilities in One Interface :** If an interface mixes unrelated actions (like *Print*(), *Scan*(), and *Fax*() in the same place), chances are some classes don't need all of them.

🔍 **Developers Keep Splitting or Commenting Out Methods :** When devs frequently edit interfaces just to avoid breaking things, or comment out method bodies – it's a sign the interface is too fat.

Real-World Analogy: Choose What You Need – Not Everything!

1. All-in-One Remote vs Custom Buttons

Imagine you're handed a giant remote control with 50 buttons — but you only ever use power, volume, and channel.
The rest? Useless, confusing, and just make it harder to find what you really need.
Now imagine a custom remote with just the buttons you actually use. Much better, right?

Fat interfaces are like those giant remotes — they force classes to deal with things they don't care about.

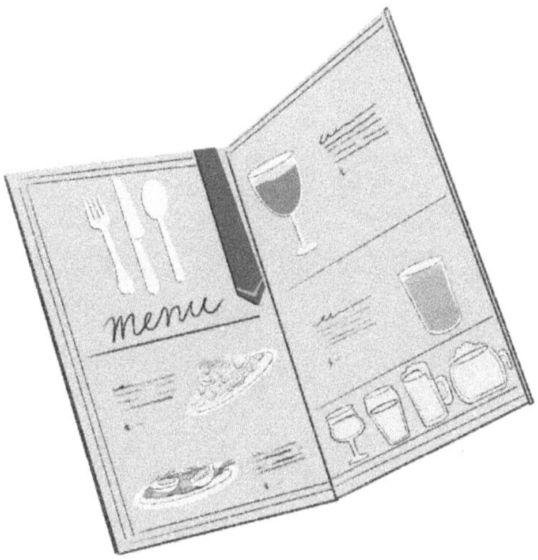

2. A Restaurant Menu with Too Many Options

You walk into a restaurant at breakfast time and they give you a menu with everything from sushi to burgers to lasagna to goat to cheese & ice cream.
You're overwhelmed, and most of it doesn't even apply to your taste.
Now imagine a focused breakfast menu — just what you need, nothing more.

Interfaces should be focused too — specific to what a class needs to do, nothing extra.

3.The Giant Swiss Army Knife

You get a giant Swiss Army Knife as a gift — it has scissors, screwdriver, magnifying glass, bottle opener, wrench, saw, pen, and even a compass.
But guess what?
You just wanted a simple screwdriver to fix your glasses.
Now you're fumbling with this bulky tool, flipping through parts you don't need.

Interfaces should be like tools: small, focused, and purpose-driven. Don't give every class the entire toolbox when they only need a screwdriver.

Deep Dive: ISP in Action

Example#1: Document Printer – The Problem

Let's say you design an interface for a multi-function printer with *Print()*, *Fax()* and *Scan()* Methods. This works fine for **advanced printers.**
But what if you build a basic printer that only prints? You're forced to implement *Fax()* and *Scan()* methods — even if they do nothing or throw exceptions.

Bad Practice: Violating ISP

Single Interface for all Methods.

```
public interface IMachine
{
    void Print(Document doc);
    void Fax(Document doc);
    void Scan(Document doc);
}
```

Why does this violate ISP?

- This violates ISP because the class is forced to depend on methods it doesn't need.

```
public class OldPrinter : IMachine
{
    public void Print(Document doc)
    {
        Console.WriteLine("Printing document...");
    }

    public void Fax(Document doc)
    {
        throw new NotImplementedException(); // ✕
    }

    public void Scan(Document doc)
    {
        throw new NotImplementedException(); // ✕
    }
}
```

Good Practice: ISP to the Rescue

Break down the fat interface into smaller, more focused interfaces:
Step 1: Split the Interface

```
public interface IPrinter
{
    void Print(Document doc);
}

public interface IScanner
{
    void Scan(Document doc);
}

public interface IFax
{
    void Fax(Document doc);
}
```

Step 2: Use Only What You Need

Now, classes only implement what they actually support.

```
public class SimplePrinter : IPrinter
{
    public void Print(Document doc)
    {
        Console.WriteLine("Printing...");
    }
}
```

```
public class AdvancedPrinter : IPrinter, IScanner, IFax
{
    public void Print(Document doc) { /* ... */ }
    public void Scan(Document doc) { /* ... */ }
    public void Fax(Document doc) { /* ... */ }
}
```

Step 3: Using the Classes in Main

Let's see how you can use the classes in your program:

```
Document doc = new Document();

SimplePrinter basicPrinter = new SimplePrinter();
basicPrinter.Print(doc); // ■ Only print - nothing else required

AdvancedPrinter smartPrinter = new AdvancedPrinter();
smartPrinter.Print(doc);
smartPrinter.Scan(doc);
smartPrinter.Fax(doc);
```

You can also use interfaces to work with different implementations:

```
IPrinter printer = new SimplePrinter();
printer.Print(doc); // Interface-based programming for flexibility!
```

● Quick Note: Why Interface-Based Programming is Flexible

Interface-based programming lets you write code that depends on behavior, not specific implementations.
■ That means:

- You can swap implementations without changing the core logic.
- You can add new classes with different behavior without touching old code.
- You can test easily by mocking interfaces.

✏ Example:

```
IPrinter printer = new SimplePrinter();
printer.Print(doc);
```

Later, if you want to use an advanced printer:

```
printer = new AdvancedPrinter();
printer.Print(doc);  // Still works!
```

■ Same code, different result.
That's the power of flexibility with interfaces! 🙌

Why is this a good practice?

- **Cleaner design** – Classes only depend on what they actually need.
- **Flexible & Extendable** – New classes can implement just the required features.
- **Better readability & maintainability** – No empty or unused methods cluttering your code.
- **Fewer bugs** – You avoid runtime errors like *NotImplementedException*.

By keeping interfaces focused and specific, your system becomes easier to understand, change, and scale..

Example#2: Smart Home Devices - The Problem
Imagine you design a smart home interface.

Bad Practice: Violating ISP
One Interface for All Devices

```
public interface ISmartDevice
{
    void TurnOn();
    void TurnOff();
    void PlayMusic();
    void SetTemperature(int degrees);
}
```

Now, you create two devices:

```
public class SmartSpeaker : ISmartDevice
{
    public void TurnOn() => Console.WriteLine("Speaker
On");
    public void TurnOff() => Console.WriteLine("Speaker
Off");
    public void PlayMusic() => Console.WriteLine("Playing
music");
    public void SetTemperature(int degrees)
    {
        // Not applicable!
        throw new NotImplementedException("Speaker can't
set temperature");
    }
}
```

```
public class SmartThermostat : ISmartDevice
{
    public void TurnOn() =>
Console.WriteLine("Thermostat On");
    public void TurnOff() =>
Console.WriteLine("Thermostat Off");
    public void PlayMusic()
    {
        // Not applicable!
        throw new NotImplementedException("Thermostat
can't play music");
    }
    public void SetTemperature(int degrees) =>
Console.WriteLine($"Set to {degrees}°C");
}
```

Why does this violate ISP?
- Both devices are forced to implement methods they don't need. This violates ISP and makes code fragile.

Good Practice: ISP to the Rescue
Break down the fat interface into smaller, more focused interfaces:

Step 1: Split the Interface

```
public interface IOnOffDevice
{
    void TurnOn();
    void TurnOff();
}

public interface IMusicPlayer
{
    void PlayMusic();
}

public interface ITemperatureControl
{
    void SetTemperature(int degrees);
}
```

Step 2: Use Only What You Need

Now your classes are clean.

```
public class SmartSpeaker : IOnOffDevice, IMusicPlayer
{
    public void TurnOn() => Console.WriteLine("Speaker On");
    public void TurnOff() => Console.WriteLine("Speaker Off");
    public void PlayMusic() => Console.WriteLine("Playing music");
}
```

```
public class SmartThermostat : IOnOffDevice, ITemperatureControl
{
    public void TurnOn() => Console.WriteLine("Thermostat On");
    public void TurnOff() => Console.WriteLine("Thermostat Off");
    public void SetTemperature(int degrees) => Console.WriteLine($"Set
to {degrees}°C");
}
```

Step 3: Call It in Main

```
ISmartSpeaker speaker = new SmartSpeaker();
speaker.TurnOn();
speaker.PlayMusic();
speaker.TurnOff();

ISmartThermostat thermostat = new SmartThermostat();
thermostat.TurnOn();
thermostat.SetTemperature(22);
thermostat.TurnOff();
```

Why is this a good practice?

- **No More Unused Code:** Classes only implement methods they actually need. No more dummy implementations!
- **Simpler and Focused Interfaces:** Easy to understand, easy to maintain.
- **Avoids Fragility:** Changes in one interface don't accidentally break other classes.
- **Better Scalability:** You can easily plug and play different devices without modifying other parts.

Conclusion

The Interface Segregation Principle is all about respecting boundaries — giving classes only what they need, and nothing more.

By keeping interfaces small and focused:

- We reduce the risk of breaking classes when interfaces change.
- Our classes remain **cleaner, simpler, and easier to test.**
- We avoid "fat" interfaces that force classes to implement useless methods.
- Future updates become smoother — no ripple effects on unrelated classes!

In short, **ISP helps us write flexible and maintainable code** by promoting the idea:

"Don't force me to do things I don't care about!"

Stick to what matters. Keep your interfaces lean. And your code will thank you later!

Now Your Turn!

Exercise 1 — Refactor the Code

Problem 1: Media Player Interface

You're given this interface:

```
public interface IMediaPlayer
{
    void PlayAudio();
    void PlayVideo();
    void RecordAudio();
    void RecordVideo();
}
```

And two classes:

```
public class AudioPlayer : IMediaPlayer
{
    public void PlayAudio() { /* logic to play audio */ }

    public void PlayVideo() { throw new NotImplementedException(); }

    public void RecordAudio() { throw new NotImplementedException(); }

    public void RecordVideo() { throw new NotImplementedException(); }
}

public class VideoRecorder : IMediaPlayer
{
    public void PlayAudio() { throw new NotImplementedException(); }

    public void PlayVideo() { throw new NotImplementedException(); }

    public void RecordAudio() { /* logic to record audio */ }

    public void RecordVideo() { /* logic to record video */ }
}
```

✎Task:

1. What problems do you notice in this design?
2. How does this violate the Interface Segregation Principle?
3. Refactor the code using smaller interfaces so each class only implements what it needs.

Problem 2: Smart Appliance Manager – Principle Mayhem

You're given this interface:

```
public interface ISmartAppliance
{
    void TurnOn();
    void TurnOff();
    void ConnectToWiFi();
    void PlayMusic();
    void DisplayContent();
}

public class SmartLight : ISmartAppliance
{
    public void TurnOn() => Console.WriteLine("Light On");
    public void TurnOff() => Console.WriteLine("Light Off");
    public void ConnectToWiFi() => Console.WriteLine("Light connected to WiFi");

    public void PlayMusic()
    {
        throw new NotImplementedException();
    }

    public void DisplayContent()
    {
        throw new NotImplementedException();
    }
}

public class ApplianceController
{
    public void Control(ISmartAppliance appliance)
    {
        appliance.TurnOn();
        appliance.ConnectToWiFi();
        appliance.PlayMusic(); // Oops: Light can't play music
    }
}
```

What's Wrong Here?

This class breaks multiple principles:

1. SRP Violation – *ApplianceController* handles turning on devices and playing music — doing too many things.
2. ISP Violation – *SmartLight* is forced to implement *PlayMusic()* and *DisplayContent()*, which don't apply.
3. OCP Violation – *ApplianceController* uses *ISmartAppliance* assuming all appliances support music. Adding a new type (e.g., SmartOven) means changing existing logic.
4. LSP Violation – Substituting *SmartLight* in *Control()* causes a runtime error because *PlayMusic()* throws an exception.

Task:

Refactor the code using proper abstractions to fix all the above principle violations. Split the interfaces where necessary, ensure substitutable behavior, and design the controller to be open for extension, closed for modification.

Exercise 2 — Match the Concept

Match with the correct answer.

Concept	Explanation
1. Interface Segregation Principle	A. When a class implements unnecessary methods
2. Fat Interface	B. Classes shouldn't be forced to depend on methods they don't use
3. Code Smell	C. Classes forced to implement unnecessary methods
4. Violation of ISP	D. Small, focused interfaces with specific responsibilities
5. Segregated Interfaces	E. Interface that has too many methods

Exercise 3 — Fill in the Blanks

Fill in the blanks with the correct terms:

1. ISP stands for ________.
2. A class should not be forced to implement methods it does not ________.
3. Creating smaller, specific interfaces improves code ________ and ________.
4. A ________ interface contains unrelated responsibilities bundled together.
5. ________ programming helps achieve loose coupling using interfaces.

Exercise 4 — Match the Concept

1. What is the main idea behind ISP?

A) Interfaces should be large and detailed
B) Classes should depend only on interfaces they actually use
C) Subclasses should override all methods
D) Classes should inherit multiple classes

2. What is a Fat Interface?

A) Interface with too many methods, causing classes to implement unnecessary ones
B) Interface that's optimized for speed
C) Interface related to memory management
D) Interface that increases performance

3. Which principle encourages creating small, specific interfaces?

A) Single Responsibility Principle
B) Interface Segregation Principle
C) Dependency Inversion Principle
D) Liskov Substitution Principle

Interview Questions for ISP

. What is the Interface Segregation Principle (ISP)?

◆ **Answer:** ISP states that a class should never be forced to implement methods it does not use.

. Why is violating ISP a problem?

◆ **Answer:** It leads to bloated classes, unnecessary dependencies, and fragile code.

. How do you fix a fat interface?

◆ **Answer:** Break it down into smaller, more specific interfaces based on different responsibilities.

. Can a class implement multiple interfaces?

◆ **Answer:** Yes! A class can implement multiple interfaces to pick only the behaviors it needs.

. How does ISP help in real-world software design?

◆ **Answer:** It makes systems easier to understand, extend, and maintain without breaking existing code.

. What is a "fat" interface?

◆ **Answer:** An interface with too many unrelated methods, forcing classes to implement unnecessary ones.

. How does ISP help with Dependency Injection and Testing?

◆ **Answer:** Small, focused interfaces allow injecting only what a class truly needs, making unit testing easier and mocking simpler.

. How does ISP relate to Single Responsibility Principle (SRP)?

◆ **Answer:** ISP ensures interfaces have a single purpose, just like SRP ensures classes have one reason to change.

. If two classes share only a few methods, should you create a common interface? Why or why not?

◆ **Answer:** Only if the shared behavior is meaningful and logical. Otherwise, forcing an interface just for a few methods can make the design worse.

10. **Can you achieve ISP without interfaces?**

◆ **Answer:** It's hard. Interfaces or abstract classes are usually needed to properly apply ISP.

Chapter 6

Dependency Inversion Principle (DIP)

What is DIP?

The **Dependency Inversion Principle (DIP)** says:

> ***High-level modules (main logic) should not depend directly on low-level modules (details like databases, APIs). Both should depend on abstractions (like interfaces or abstract classes).***

It also says that: *Abstractions should not depend on details. Details should depend on abstractions.*

Are you worried that this definition is using complex words which is against the concept of this book ?

Don't worry — we'll break it down together in the simplest way possible, just like we've done throughout this book!

👉 ***Abstractions should not depend on details***

→ Interfaces or abstract classes (the "abstractions") should not know anything about how the actual work (details) is done.

→ They should just define what needs to be done, not how.

Example:

- An interface *ILogger* just says: *"There is a Log() method."*
- It doesn't care if the log is saved to a file, database, or sent to an API.

👉 ***Details should depend on abstractions***

→ The real working classes (details) like *FileLogger* or *DatabaseLogger* should be built based on the interface.

→ They follow what the interface says.

Example:

- *FileLogger* implements the *ILogger* interface and writes to a file.
- *DatabaseLogger* also implements *ILogger*, but writes to a database.

● In short:

- Big boss (abstraction) just says "I want logging."
- Workers (details) say "Okay, we will log it however you want."
- Big boss doesn't care how it's done!

Why DIP Matters

Imagine building a tall tower using blocks.
If you place heavy blocks directly on weak ones, the whole tower becomes unstable.
Similarly, if your high-level code depends too much on low-level details, a small change in the details can break everything above it.
When you follow DIP, your code becomes:
■ Flexible – Easy to swap low-level modules without changing the core logic.
■ Testable – You can test parts separately using mocks or stubs.
■ Maintainable – Updating a small detail won't shake your entire project!
In short: Strong foundation, strong software. 🏗️✨

Neglecting the Dependency Inversion Principle can lead to several issues:

- **Tight Coupling:** High-level modules become dependent on low-level modules, making the system rigid and hard to modify.
- **Difficult Testing:** Without abstractions, substituting components for testing purposes becomes challenging.
- **Limited Reusability:** High-level modules tied to specific implementations can't be easily reused in different contexts.
- **Increased Maintenance Effort:** Changes in low-level modules may require modifications in high-level modules, increasing the maintenance burden.

When DIP is Broken: Common Signs

How do you know if your code is violating the Dependency Inversion Principle? Look out for these signs:

● **High-level modules directly create or control low-level modules.**
If a high-level class (the one containing important business logic) is responsible for creating or managing low-level details (like database connections, file readers, or API calls), it means the system is tightly coupled. This makes the code rigid and hard to adapt to changes.

● **Changes in low-level details ripple through the entire system**.
Whenever you change how a database, a file, or a network call works, and you find yourself updating a lot of classes everywhere, it shows a strong dependency on implementation details rather than abstractions.

● **Hard-to-test code because of tight coupling.**
If your classes directly depend on external systems (like databases or web services) without using interfaces, you'll find it very hard to write unit tests. You might be forced to set up the whole environment just to test a tiny piece of code.

● **Excessive use of new keywords scattered around.**
If everywhere in your code you see new SomeClass(), it means classes are manually constructing their dependencies. Instead, they should rely on abstractions provided from outside (through constructor or setter injection).

● **Adding or modifying a feature often leads to breaking the existing system.**
If simple feature updates require modifying multiple unrelated classes, it's a clear sign that your system is fragile and not following DIP. A change in low-level details should never affect high-level modules if abstractions are respected.

Real-World Analogy: Relax at the Top, Hustle at the Bottom!

1. Wall Chargers and Mobile Phones

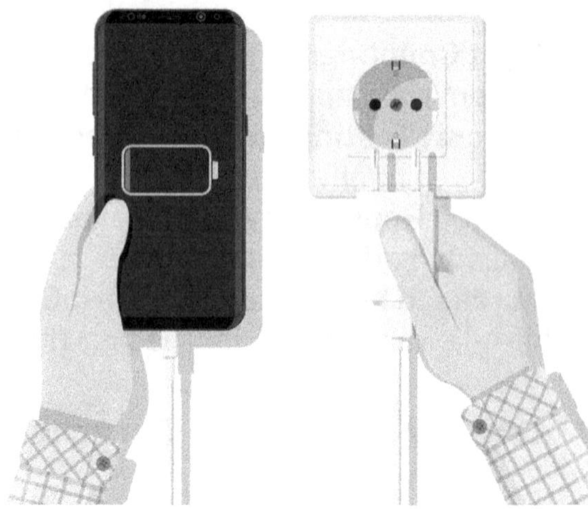

Most modern smartphones (iPhone, Android, etc.) use standard charging cables like USB-C or Lightning.
The charger doesn't need to know which phone it is — as long as the connector matches the interface, it works!
Here, the charger (high-level device) depends on a standard cable design, not on the internal battery system of each phone.

■ **When devices rely on standard connectors (abstractions), they can work together without knowing each other's details.**

2. Wall Sockets and Appliances

Wall sockets don't care whether you plug in a mobile charger, a vacuum cleaner, or a toaster.
They all use the same standard plug interface.
The electricity provider (high-level system) depends on a common socket design — not on the details of each device.

■ **When systems depend on shared interfaces, they stay flexible and don't break when devices change.**

3. Online Payment Systems

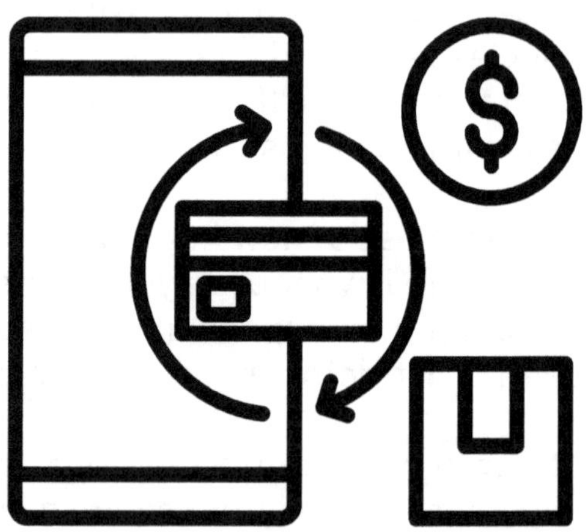

An e-commerce website accepts payments through credit cards, PayPal, or digital wallets.
But the website doesn't worry about how each method processes the payment internally.
It simply calls a *PaymentProcessor* interface, and the specific payment methods handle the details.
The website (high-level system) depends on the abstraction, not the specific payment method details.

■ **High-level modules should trust a shared contract, not how every payment method does its job.**

> **Relax at the Top, Hustle at the Bottom!**
> **High-level modules should stay relaxed, focusing only on "what" needs to happen.**
> **The low-level details should hustle in the background to make it happen, without disturbing the upper layers!**

Deep Dive: DIP in Action

Example#1: Simple Notification System

Suppose we're building a simple notification system:

Bad Practice: Violating DIP

```
public class EmailService
{
    public void SendEmail(string message)
    {
        Console.WriteLine("Sending EMAIL: " + message);
    }
}

public class NotificationManager
{
    private EmailService _emailService;

    public NotificationManager()
    {
        _emailService = new EmailService();
    }

    public void NotifyUser(string message)
    {
        _emailService.SendEmail(message);
    }
}
```

Why does this violate DIP?

- *NotificationManager* is tightly coupled to *EmailService.*
- If we want to switch to SMS or push notifications, we have to modify *NotificationManager,* violating OCP.
- Also, *NotificationManager* (high-level) is depending on a concrete *EmailService* (low-level), violating DIP.

Good Practice: DIP to the Rescue

Step 1: Introduce an Abstraction

Let's introduce an interface that all messaging services can implement:

```
public interface IMessageService
{
    void Send(string message);
}
```

Now let's have EmailService implement it:

```
public class EmailService : IMessageService
{
    public void Send(string message)
    {
        Console.WriteLine("Sending EMAIL: " + message);
    }
}
```

We can add other services too:

```
public class SmsService : IMessageService
{
    public void Send(string message)
    {
        Console.WriteLine("Sending SMS: " + message);
    }
}
```

Step 2: Invert the Dependency in the High-Level Class

Now, the high-level class depends on the abstraction, not the concrete class:

```
public class NotificationManager
{
    private readonly IMessageService _messageService;

    public NotificationManager(IMessageService messageService)
    {
        _messageService = messageService;
    }

    public void NotifyUser(string message)
    {
        _messageService.Send(message);
    }
}
```

Step 3: Using It in Main (Flexible Dependency Injection)

```
class Program
{
    static void Main()
    {
        IMessageService service = new EmailService(); // Or new SmsService();
        NotificationManager manager = new NotificationManager(service);

        manager.NotifyUser("Welcome to our system!");
    }
}
```

Why is this a good practice?

- **Flexible:** We can inject any message service without changing *NotificationManager*.
- **Testable:** Easily mock *IMessageService* for unit testing.
- **Scalable:** Add WhatsApp, Push Notification, etc., without modifying core logic.
- **Decoupled:** High-level modules are independent of low-level implementation details.

What is Dependency Injection?

Dependency Injection is a way to give an object the things (dependencies) it needs — *from the outside* — instead of letting the object create them itself.

Think of it like this:

👉 Instead of a class saying, *"I'll go get my tools,"*
it says, *"Hey, give me the tools I need."*

This helps keep code flexible, testable, and decoupled.

Example#2: Logging System

Imagine you're building a system where different components need to log messages (errors, info, etc.).

Bad Practice: Violating DIP

```
public class FileLogger
{
    public void Log(string message)
    {
        Console.WriteLine("Writing to file: " + message);
    }
}

public class OrderProcessor
{
    private FileLogger logger = new FileLogger();

    public void ProcessOrder()
    {
        // Process the order
        logger.Log("Order processed.");
    }
}
```

Why does this violate DIP?

- *OrderProcessor* (high-level module) is directly dependent on *FileLogger* (low-level module).
- If we want to log to a database, console, or cloud logger, we'll have to modify *OrderProcessor* — breaking the Open/Closed Principle too.
- It's hard to test *OrderProcessor* without creating a *FileLogger*.

Good Practice: DIP to the Rescue

Step 1: Introduce an Abstraction

Let's introduce an interface that all messaging services can implement:

```
public interface ILogger
{
    void Log(string message);
}
```

Step 2: Implement multiple loggers

```
public class FileLogger : ILogger
{
    public void Log(string message)
    {
        Console.WriteLine("Writing to file: " + message);
    }
}

public class ConsoleLogger : ILogger
{
    public void Log(string message)
    {
        Console.WriteLine("Console log: " + message);
    }
}
```

Step 3: Inject the logger into the processor

```
public class OrderProcessor
{
    private readonly ILogger logger;

    public OrderProcessor(ILogger logger)
    {
        this.logger = logger;
    }

    public void ProcessOrder()
    {
        // Process the order
        logger.Log("Order processed.");
    }
}
```

Step 4: Call it from Main

```
class Program
{
    static void Main()
    {
        ILogger logger = new ConsoleLogger(); // or new FileLogger()
        OrderProcessor processor = new OrderProcessor(logger);
        processor.ProcessOrder();
    }
}
```

Why is this a good practice?

- You can easily swap loggers (file, console, database) without touching *OrderProcessor*.
- Encourages flexibility, testability, and clean architecture.
- *OrderProcessor* now depends on an abstraction (*ILogger*), not a detail (*FileLogger*) — which is the core idea of DIP.

Conclusion

The **Dependency Inversion Principle** flips the traditional flow of dependencies. Instead of high-level modules being tightly coupled to low-level details, both sides depend on abstractions — making your code flexible, testable, and future-proof.

When DIP is followed:

- High-level modules (like *OrderProcessor*) don't care how the work is done — they only care that it gets done.
- Low-level modules (like *FileLogger*, *EmailSender*, etc.) can evolve independently, without breaking core business logic.
- Testing becomes much easier because you can inject mock implementations.
- You follow Open/Closed Principle naturally, since adding new behaviors doesn't require modifying existing classes.

Think of DIP as the principle that allows your software to talk to interfaces, not implementations — leading to clean architecture and happy developers. ●

Now Your Turn!

Exercise 1 Refactor the Code

Problem 1: Payment Processing System

You are given the following code:

```
public class CreditCardProcessor
{
    public void ProcessPayment(double amount)
    {
        Console.WriteLine("Processing credit card payment of $" + amount);
    }
}

public class CheckoutService
{
    private CreditCardProcessor _processor = new CreditCardProcessor();

    public void Checkout(double totalAmount)
    {
        _processor.ProcessPayment(totalAmount);
    }
}
```

✎Task:

1. Identify how this violates the Dependency Inversion Principle.
2. Refactor this code to follow DIP using an interface-based design, so that other payment methods (e.g., PayPal, UPI) can also be used in future without changing *CheckoutService*.

Problem 2: Order Management System – A Tangle of Responsibilities

You are given the following code:

```
public class OrderManager
{
    public void PlaceOrder(string productId, int quantity)
    {
        Console.WriteLine("Placing order for " + productId + " with quantity " + quantity);

        // Save order to database
        Console.WriteLine("Saving order to database...");

        // Send confirmation email
        Console.WriteLine("Sending confirmation email to customer...");

        // Process payment using a fixed method
        Console.WriteLine("Processing payment using Credit Card...");
    }
}
```

🔍 **What's Wrong?**

❌ Single Responsibility Principle (SRP) Violation

OrderManager is doing too many things:

- Order placement logic
- Saving to database
- Sending email
- Payment processing

❌ Open/Closed Principle (OCP) Violation

Want to change the payment method? Or switch email providers? You'll have to modify this class.

❌ Liskov Substitution Principle (LSP) Violation (Future Risk)

If we inherit *OrderManager* in the future for a different type of order (e.g., digital download), and override *PlaceOrder*() but skip database or payment logic, it would violate LSP.

❌ Dependency Inversion Principle (DIP) Violation

OrderManager depends on concrete implementations:

- A specific payment method (Credit Card)
- Email is tightly embedded
- No abstraction layers

✏️Task for the Readers:

Refactor this tangled mess to follow all four violated principles:

- Break responsibilities into separate classes/interfaces.
- Use abstractions for payment and notification logic.
- Make it extensible and testable.
- Keep *OrderManager* focused only on coordinating the order workflow.

Exercise 2 Match the Concept

Draw a line between each concept on the left with its correct description on the right.

Concept	Description
1. Dependency Inversion	A. Allows high-level modules to work with any implementation
2. Interface	B. A design that breaks if you change from one class to another
3. Tight Coupling	C. When classes are hard-wired to each other's implementation
4. Abstraction	D. Principle where high-level modules should not depend on low-level modules
5. Constructor Injection	E. A common way to pass dependencies using class constructors

Exercise 3 — Fill in the Blanks

Fill in the blanks with the correct terms below:

1. High-level modules should not depend on ________________.
2. Both high-level and low-level modules should depend on ___________.
3. Abstractions should not depend on _________.
4. ______ should depend on abstractions.
5. ______________ is a way to provide dependencies from the outside.
6. Without DIP, code becomes __________ and harder to maintain.
7. DIP helps in writing code that is __________ and ____________.
8. Interfaces and abstract classes are examples of ____________.
9. A common sign of DIP violation is the use of the ______ keyword inside classes for creating dependencies.
10. Using ________________ makes it clear what a class depends on.

Exercise 4 — Match the Concept

1. What is the main goal of the Dependency Inversion Principle?
A) To reduce the number of classes in a project
B) To eliminate the need for inheritance
C) To decouple high-level modules from low-level implementations
D) To improve runtime performance

2. Which of the following best supports the Dependency Inversion Principle?
A) Instantiating objects using the new keyword inside classes
B) Directly using concrete classes in high-level modules
C) Depending on abstractions like interfaces or abstract classes
D) Hardcoding dependencies into utility classes

Interview Questions for DIP

. What is the Dependency Inversion Principle, and why is it important?

◆ **Answer:** DIP encourages high-level modules to depend on abstractions, not concrete implementations, promoting decoupling and flexibility.

. Can you give a real-life analogy to explain DIP?

◆ **Answer:** Examples like wall sockets and appliances, payment systems with different gateways, etc.

. How does DIP differ from Dependency Injection?

◆ **Answer:** DIP is a design principle; Dependency Injection is a design pattern used to implement it.

. What problems can occur if high-level modules depend directly on low-level details?

◆ **Answer:** Rigid code, hard to test, poor scalability, tightly coupled modules.

. How would you refactor a tightly coupled class to follow DIP?

◆ **Answer:** Introduce an interface/abstract class and inject the dependency via constructor or setter.

. Which SOLID principles does DIP often work closely with, and how?

◆ **Answer:** *OCP*: Because it allows changes through abstraction without modifying core logic. *SRP*: Because it keeps concerns separate (e.g., logic vs. implementation details).

. What are some signs that your code is violating DIP?

◆ **Answer:** High-level classes directly instantiate or control low-level classes.

- Changes in low-level modules force changes in high-level logic.
- Unit testing is hard due to tight coupling.
- Frequent new keyword usage scattered across the code.

. How does applying DIP make your code more testable?

◆ **Answer:** Because you depend on abstractions, you can easily swap real implementations with mocks or stubs during testing without modifying the core logic.

. Can you violate DIP even if you're using interfaces?

◆ **Answer:** Yes, if the high-level module is still responsible for creating the concrete implementation (e.g., using new *ConcreteClass()*), it's still coupled to the detail and DIP is violated.

10. **What is the role of the Inversion of Control (IoC) container in DIP?**

◆ **Answer:** An IoC container helps manage dependency injection automatically, wiring dependencies at runtime based on configuration or metadata, thus supporting DIP implementation.

A QUICK RECAP OF EACH SOLID PRINCIPLE

S — Single Responsibility Principle (SRP) – "One Job Only"

Ask yourself:

- Does this class do more than one job?
- Does it change for more than one reason?
- Is it handling logic + data access + UI?

Common signs of violation:

- Large classes with "Manager", "Processor", or "Helper" in the name
- Multiple if-else handling unrelated tasks
- A class doing calculations AND saving to DB

O — Open/Closed Principle (OCP) – "Extend, Don't Modify"

Ask yourself:

- Do I need to modify existing classes to add new features?
- Can I extend behavior without touching old code?

Common signs of violation:

- Long *switch* or *if-else* blocks for types or actions
- Rewriting logic in base classes for new scenarios
- Frequent edits to tested, working code

L — Liskov Substitution Principle (LSP) – "No Surprises"

Ask yourself:

- Can I use a subclass wherever the base class is expected — without surprises?
- Does the subclass follow the *behavior contract*?

Common signs of violation:

- Subclass throws *NotImplementedException*
- Overridden method changes behavior completely
- A method in base class doesn't make sense for all subclasses.

I — Interface Segregation Principle (ISP) – "No Unnecessary Dependencies"

Ask yourself:

- Is this interface too big?
- Are some classes forced to implement methods they don't use?

Common signs of violation:

- Interface has unrelated responsibilities (e.g., *IPrinter* with *Fax()*)
- Empty method implementations in a class.
- Fat interfaces reused by unrelated classes.

D — Dependency Inversion Principle (DIP) – "Depend on Abstractions"

Ask yourself:

- Are high-level classes depending on low-level implementations?
- Can I swap a dependency without rewriting the class?

Common signs of violation:

- Using *new* to create concrete classes in main logic.
- High-level modules know too much about low-level details.
- No use of interfaces or abstractions.

Quick Use Case Guide

Principle	What You Should Do	What You Need to Avoid
SRP	Keep classes focused	Mixing responsibilities
OCP	Extend, not modify	Editing working code
LSP	Respect behavior contracts	Forcing subclasses to behave differently
ISP	Split big interfaces	Making "God" interfaces
DIP	Depend on abstractions	Tightly coupling with concrete classes

ANSWERS

Exercise 1 — Refactor the Code

Problem 1: Order Processing Mess

Refactored code following SRP:

```
class OrderProcessor {
    public void ProcessOrder(string orderId) {
        Console.WriteLine($"Processing order {orderId}");
    }
}

class PaymentProcessor {
    public void MakePayment(string orderId, double amount) {
        Console.WriteLine($"Processing payment of ${amount} for order {orderId}");
    }
}

class InvoiceGenerator {
    public void GenerateInvoice(string orderId) {
        Console.WriteLine($"Generating invoice for order {orderId}");
    }
}
```

■ Order processing, payment, and invoicing are now handled by separate classes.

Problem 2: The Overcomplicated Logger

Refactored code following SRP:

```
class Logger {
    public void LogMessage(string message) {
        Console.WriteLine($"Logging message: {message}");
    }
}

class EmailNotifier {
    public void SendEmailAlert(string message) {
        Console.WriteLine($"Sending email alert: {message}");
    }
}
```

■ Logging and email notifications are now separate responsibilities.

Problem 3: The Overloaded Employee Class

Refactored code following SRP:

```
class Employee {
    public string Name { get; set; }
}

class SalaryCalculator {
    public void CalculateSalary(Employee employee) {
        Console.WriteLine($"Calculating salary for {employee.Name}");
    }
}

class EmailNotifier {
    public void SendEmailNotification(Employee employee) {
        Console.WriteLine($"Sending email to {employee.Name}");
    }
}
```

■ Employee details, salary calculation, and email notifications are now handled separately.

Exercise 2 Match the Concept

1. **C - Break it into smaller classes**
2. **A - Separate concerns properly**
3. **B - Keep responsibilities isolated**

Exercise 3 Fill in the Blanks

1. SRP states that a class should have only **one** reason(s) to change.
2. Breaking SRP improves **maintainability** and **readability** of the code.
3. A **God** class is one that handles multiple concerns instead of just one.

Exercise 4 Multiple Choice Questions (MCQs)

. C) To ensure each class has only one reason to change

2. B) A class that both calculates salary and sends salary emails

Exercise 1 — Refactor the Code

Problem 1: Discount & Invoice Generation

Refactored code following SRP and OCP:

```
public interface IDiscountStrategy
{
    double ApplyDiscount(double price);
}

public class RegularCustomerDiscount : IDiscountStrategy
{
    public double ApplyDiscount(double price) => price * 0.05;
}

public class PremiumCustomerDiscount : IDiscountStrategy
{
    public double ApplyDiscount(double price) => price * 0.10;
}

public class Invoice
{
    private readonly IDiscountStrategy _discountStrategy;

    public Invoice(IDiscountStrategy discountStrategy)
    {
        _discountStrategy = discountStrategy;
    }

    public double CalculateTotal(double price, int quantity)
    {
        double discount = _discountStrategy.ApplyDiscount(price);
        double total = (price * quantity) - discount;
        Console.WriteLine("Invoice Generated: " + total);
        return total;
    }
}
```

■ Adding a new Discount will not affect other code.

Problem 2: Area Calculator

The following follows OCP:

```
public abstract class Shape{
    public abstract double CalculateArea();
}
public class Circle : Shape{
    public double Radius { get; set; }
    public override double CalculateArea() => Math.PI * Radius * Radius;
}
public class Rectangle : Shape{
    public double Width { get; set; }
    public double Height { get; set; }
    public override double CalculateArea() => Width * Height;
}
public class AreaCalculator{
    public double CalculateArea(Shape shape) => shape.CalculateArea();
}
```

■ Adding a new Shape will not affect code for other shapes.

Exercise 2 Match the Concept

1. **C - Existing code should remain unchanged while allowing extensions.**
2. **A - Using if-else conditions to handle new cases instead of extending behavior.**
3. **B - Applying abstraction and polymorphism to allow future extensions.**

Exercise 3 Fill in the Blanks

1. OCP states that a class should be **open** for extension but **closed** for modification.
2. The key technique to implement OCP is using **abstraction** and **polymorphism** instead of modifying existing code.
3. Using a **base** class allows behavior to be extended without changing base logic.

Exercise 4 Multiple Choice Questions (MCQs)

. **B**) Adding new conditions inside an existing method

2. **C**) Strategy

Exercise 1 Refactor the Code

Problem 1: Report Generator

<u>Original Problem Recap:</u> The *ReadOnlyReport* class overrides *Generate()* and throws an exception.

So, substituting *ReadOnlyReport* in place of *Report* breaks the Liskov Substitution Principle.

❌ <u>Why it breaks LSP:</u>

Because the child class (*ReadOnlyReport*) changes the behavior of its parent (*Report*) by throwing an exception instead of doing what *Generate()* is expected to do. So, using a *ReadOnlyReport* where a *Report* is expected results in a failure.

Refactored Solution:

We separate the two responsibilities into interfaces:

```
public interface IReport
{
    void Generate();
}

public interface IReadOnlyReport
{
    void Display();
}
```

Now we implement them:

```
public class EditableReport : IReport
{
    public void Generate()
    {
        Console.WriteLine("Generating editable report...");
    }
}

public class ReadOnlyReport : IReadOnlyReport
{
    public void Display()
    {
        Console.WriteLine("Displaying read-only report...");
    }
}
```

Result:

Now, there's no broken substitution. Each class follows LSP by only implementing the behavior it supports. Clients who need to generate reports use *IReport*. Clients who just need to view can use *IReadOnlyReport*.

Problem 2: Manage User Class

<u>Original Problem Recap:</u> The *GuestUser* class inherits from *User*, but it throws an exception when trying to send a welcome email.

❌ <u>LSP Violation</u>: *GuestUser* cannot fully behave like a *User*, because it fails when calling *SendWelcomeEmail*(). This breaks substitutability.

❌ <u>SRP Violation:</u> The User class is doing two things:

1. Handling user data
2. Sending welcome emails

This mixes two responsibilities.

■ **Refactored Solution:**

<u>Step 1: Break responsibilities</u>

Create a *WelcomeEmailSender* service:

```
public class WelcomeEmailSender
{
    public void SendEmail(User user)
    {
        Console.WriteLine($"Sending welcome email to {user.Name}");
    }
}
```

<u>Step 2: Clean user classes</u>

```
public class User
{
    public string Name { get; set; }
}

public class GuestUser : User
{
    // No email responsibility here
}
```

<u>Step 3: Use the service where needed</u>

```
var regularUser = new User { Name = "Ali" };
var guestUser = new GuestUser { Name = "Guest" };

var emailSender = new WelcomeEmailSender();
emailSender.SendEmail(regularUser); // OK
// No call for guestUser - and no exception!
```

● **Result:**

- ■ LSP fixed: GuestUser no longer overrides or misuses methods.
- ■ SRP fixed: Email logic is separated from User class.

Exercise 2 — Match the Concept

1. **B - A principle that ensures subclasses can be used in place of base classes without surprises.**
2. **C - Allows a method to be overridden in derived class**
3. **E - Used in derived class to modify base class method behavior**
4. **A - Subclass throws exception for a method in base class**
5. **D - Helps split incompatible behaviors cleanly**

Exercise 3 — Fill in the Blanks

1. The **subclass** should be replaceable by its **base class** without changing the program's expected **behavior**.
2. Violating **LSP** can result in unexpected bugs and fragile code.
3. If a subclass needs to change how a method works, it can use the **override** keyword.

Exercise 4 — Multiple Choice Questions (MCQs)

. **C)** Objects of a subclass should be replaceable for objects of a base class without affecting the program.

2. **B)** A subclass throws an exception for a method expected to work.
3. **C)** Unexpected behavior and bugs.
4. **C)** Designing subclasses that follow the contract of the base class.

Chapter 5 - Answers

Exercise 1 — Refactor the Code

Problem 1: Media Player Interface

Break the interface into smaller, more focused ones. Update the classes to implement only what they need.

```
public interface IAudioPlayable
{
    void PlayAudio();
}

public interface IVideoPlayable
{
    void PlayVideo();
}

public interface IAudioRecordable
{
    void RecordAudio();
}

public interface IVideoRecordable
{
    void RecordVideo();
}
```

```
public class AudioPlayer : IAudioPlayable
{
    public void PlayAudio()
    {
        Console.WriteLine("Playing audio...");
    }
}

public class VideoRecorder : IAudioRecordable, IVideoRecordable
{
    public void RecordAudio()
    {
        Console.WriteLine("Recording audio...");
    }

    public void RecordVideo()
    {
        Console.WriteLine("Recording video...");
    }
}
```

✸ Why This Is a Good Practice

■ Each class only implements the functionality it truly supports — no more throw new NotImplementedException()!

■ Code becomes cleaner, more maintainable, and easier to understand.

■ If requirements change later (e.g., a new SmartDevice that only plays video), we can easily reuse the relevant interfaces.

Problem 2: Smart Appliance Manager

Here's the full refactoring to fix SRP, OCP, LSP, ISP

```
// Step 1: Break the interface into
smaller, focused interfaces
public interface IConnectable
{
 void ConnectToWiFi();
}
public interface ISwitchable
{
 void TurnOn();
 void TurnOff();
}
public interface IMusicPlayer
{
 void PlayMusic();
}
public interface IDisplayDevice
{
 void DisplayContent();
}
```

```
// Step 2: Implement interfaces properly for each device
public class SmartLight : ISwitchable, IConnectable
{
    public void TurnOn() => Console.WriteLine("Light On");
    public void TurnOff() => Console.WriteLine("Light Off");
    public void ConnectToWiFi() => Console.WriteLine("Light
connected to WiFi");
}

public class SmartSpeaker : ISwitchable, IConnectable,
IMusicPlayer
{
    public void TurnOn() => Console.WriteLine("Speaker On");
    public void TurnOff() => Console.WriteLine("Speaker
Off");
    public void ConnectToWiFi() => Console.WriteLine("Speaker
connected to WiFi");
    public void PlayMusic() => Console.WriteLine("Playing
music...");
]
```

```
// Step 3: Create a controller that depends only on required interfaces
public class ApplianceController
{
    public void PowerOnDevice(ISwitchable device)
    {
        device.TurnOn();
    }

    public void ConnectDevice(IConnectable device)
    {
        device.ConnectToWiFi();
    }

    public void PlayMusicDevice(IMusicPlayer device)
    {
        device.PlayMusic();
    }
}
```

```
// Step 4: Call it from Main
class Program
{
    static void Main()
    {
        SmartLight light = new SmartLight();
        SmartSpeaker speaker = new SmartSpeaker();
        ApplianceController controller = new ApplianceController();

        controller.PowerOnDevice(light);
        controller.ConnectDevice(light);

        controller.PowerOnDevice(speaker);
        controller.ConnectDevice(speaker);
        controller.PlayMusicDevice(speaker); // Only speaker can play music
    }
}
```

⚫ How This Refactoring Solves the Problems:

SRP Fixed: *ApplianceController* now has a single responsibility for each type of action.

ISP Fixed: Devices only implement interfaces they truly need.

OCP Fixed: Adding new appliances (like SmartOven) doesn't modify existing code.

LSP Fixed: Substituting any device will not cause runtime errors anymore.

💡 Lesson Learned:

Big interfaces cause problems — keep them small and focused.

Classes should only implement what they actually need.

Code should be flexible enough to add new features without changing old code.

Always design classes and interfaces that are easy to use, extend, and trust.

Exercise 2 — Match the Concept

1. **B. Classes shouldn't be forced to depend on methods they don't use**
2. **E. Interface that has too many methods**
3. **A. When a class implements unnecessary methods**
4. **C. Classes forced to implement unnecessary methods**
5. **D. Small, focused interfaces with specific responsibilities**

Exercise 3 — Fill in the Blanks

1. ISP stands for **Interface Segregation Principle.**
2. A class should not be forced to implement methods it does not **use**.
3. Creating smaller, specific interfaces improves code **flexibility** and **readability**.
4. A **fat** interface contains unrelated responsibilities bundled together.
5. **Interface-based** programming helps achieve loose coupling using interfaces.

Exercise 4 — Multiple Choice Questions (MCQs)

. **B)** Classes should depend only on interfaces they actually use

2. **A)** Interface with too many methods, causing classes to implement unnecessary ones
3. **B)** Interface Segregation Principle.

Exercise 1 Refactor the Code

Problem 1: Applying DIP to the Payment System

Step 1: Create an Abstraction (Interface)

```
public interface IPaymentProcessor
{
    void ProcessPayment(double amount);
}
```

Step 2: Implement the Interface in Concrete Classes

```
public class CreditCardProcessor : IPaymentProcessor
{
    public void ProcessPayment(double amount)
    {
        Console.WriteLine("Processing credit card payment of $" + amount);
    }
}

public class PayPalProcessor : IPaymentProcessor
{
    public void ProcessPayment(double amount)
    {
        Console.WriteLine("Processing PayPal payment of $" + amount);
    }
}
```

Step 3: Use the Abstraction in the High-Level Class

```
public class CheckoutService
{
    private IPaymentProcessor _paymentProcessor;

    public CheckoutService(IPaymentProcessor paymentProcessor)
    {
        _paymentProcessor = paymentProcessor;
    }

    public void Checkout(double totalAmount)
    {
        _paymentProcessor.ProcessPayment(totalAmount);
    }
}
```

Step 4: Use It in Main Method

```
class Program
{
    static void Main(string[] args)
    {
        IPaymentProcessor processor = new CreditCardProcessor();
        CheckoutService checkout = new CheckoutService(processor);
        checkout.Checkout(100.0);

        // Easily switch to PayPal without changing CheckoutService
        IPaymentProcessor paypalProcessor = new PayPalProcessor();
        CheckoutService paypalCheckout = new CheckoutService(paypalProcessor);
        paypalCheckout.Checkout(250.0);
    }
}
```

Why This is a Good Practice

- The high-level module (*CheckoutService*) now depends on an abstraction, not a specific implementation.
- You can easily add new payment types (like UPI, Crypto) without modifying existing classes.
- Follows Open/Closed Principle too — the system is open for extension but closed for modification.
- Easier to test using mock implementations of *IPaymentProcessor*.

Problem 2: Applying DIP to the Order Management System

Refactored Solution: Clean & Compliant with SRP, OCP, LSP, and DIP

Step 1: Define Abstractions

```
public interface IPaymentProcessor
{
    void ProcessPayment(string productId, int quantity);
}

public interface IOrderRepository
{
    void Save(string productId, int quantity);
}

public interface INotifier
{
    void SendConfirmation(string productId);
}
```

Step 2: Implement Specific Details

```
public class CreditCardPaymentProcessor : IPaymentProcessor
{
    public void ProcessPayment(string productId, int quantity)
    {
        Console.WriteLine("Processing payment via Credit Card...");
    }
}
public class OrderDatabaseRepository : IOrderRepository
{
    public void Save(string productId, int quantity)
    {
        Console.WriteLine("Saving order to the database...");
    }
}
```

```
public class EmailNotifier : INotifier
{
    public void SendConfirmation(string productId)
    {
        Console.WriteLine("Sending confirmation email...");
    }
}
```

Step 3: Refactor *OrderManager* to use abstractions

```
public class OrderManager
{
    private readonly IPaymentProcessor _paymentProcessor;
    private readonly IOrderRepository _orderRepository;
    private readonly INotifier _notifier;

    public OrderManager(IPaymentProcessor paymentProcessor, IOrderRepository orderRepository, INotifier notifier)
    {
        _paymentProcessor = paymentProcessor;
        _orderRepository = orderRepository;
        _notifier = notifier;
    }

    public void PlaceOrder(string productId, int quantity)
    {
        Console.WriteLine($"Placing order for {productId} (Qty: {quantity})");
        _orderRepository.Save(productId, quantity);
        _paymentProcessor.ProcessPayment(productId, quantity);
        _notifier.SendConfirmation(productId);
    }
}
```

Step 4: Call from *Main()*

```
class Program
{
    static void Main()
    {
        var payment = new CreditCardPaymentProcessor();
        var repository = new OrderDatabaseRepository();
        var notifier = new EmailNotifier();

        var orderManager = new OrderManager(payment, repository, notifier);
        orderManager.PlaceOrder("Laptop", 1);
    }
}
```

● **Why This Refactor is a Good Practice:**

● **SRP:** Each class has one job only.

🔌 **OCP:** Want to add PayPal? Just implement IPaymentProcessor.

🧩 **LSP:** We can substitute any implementation without breaking expectations.

🕸 **DIP:** High-level class (OrderManager) depends on abstractions, not details.

Exercise 2 — Match the Concept

1. **D - Principle where high-level modules should not depend on low-level modules**
2. **A - Allows high-level modules to work with any implementation**
3. **C - When classes are hard-wired to each other's implementation.**
4. **B - A design that breaks if you change from one class to another.**
5. **E - A common way to pass dependencies using class constructors.**

Exercise 3 — Fill in the Blanks

1. High-level modules should not depend on **low-level modules.**
2. Both high-level and low-level modules should depend on **abstractions.**
3. Abstractions should not depend on **details**.
4. **Details** should depend on abstractions.
5. **Dependency Injection** is a way to provide dependencies from the outside.
6. Without DIP, code becomes **tightly coupled** and harder to maintain.
7. DIP helps in writing code that is **flexible** and **extensible**.
8. Interfaces and abstract classes are examples of **abstractions**.
9. A common sign of DIP violation is the use of the **new** keyword inside classes for creating dependencies.
10. Using **constructor injection** makes it clear what a class depends on.

Exercise 4 — Multiple Choice Questions (MCQs)

. **C) To decouple high-level modules from low-level implementations**

2. **C) Depending on abstractions like interfaces or abstract classes**

A Small Note from the Author

Thank you for joining me on this journey through the world of SOLID principles.
I truly hope this book made complex ideas feel simple, practical, and even a little fun. 😊
If you found this book helpful, inspiring, or even just a bit easier to understand than you expected —
please consider leaving a positive review or rating. *Your kind words help this book reach more learners like you and keep the Logic Ladder series going strong.*
Every review counts, and it means the world to indie authors like me! 🤍
Stay curious, keep building, and never stop learning.
See you in the next book! 🚀
Warm wishes,
Humna Ansari
Author of A SOLID Way in C#

www.ingramcontent.com/pod-product-compliance
Lightning Source LLC
La Vergne TN
LVHW082357200926
848481LV00012B/3596